PRESIDENTS

RUTHERFORD B. HAYES

A MyReportLinks.com Book

Ron Knapp

MyReportLinks.com Books
an imprint of
Enslow Publishers, Inc. E
Box 398, 40 Industrial Road
Berkeley Heights, NJ 07922
USA

MyReportLinks.com Books, an imprint of Enslow Publishers, Inc.

Library of Congress Cataloging-in-Publication Data

Knapp, Ron
  Rutherford B. Hayes : A MyReportLinks.com Book / Ron Knapp.
     p. cm. — (Presidents)
  Includes bibliographical references and index.
  Contents: Struggle for survival, September 1862— 2. Formative years, 1822–1845 — 3.
New ambitions, 1850–1876— 4. Disputed election, 1876–1877— 5. A loyal American,
1877–1880.
  Summary: Examines the life and career of the Civil War general and Ohio politician who
became the nineteenth president of the United States. Includes Internet links to Web sites,
source documents, and photographs related to Rutherford B. Hayes.
  ISBN 0-7660-5010-6
  1. Hayes, Rutherford Birchard, 1822–1893—Juvenile literature. 2. Presidents—United
States—Biography—Juvenile literature. [1. Hayes, Rutherford Birchard, 1822–1893. 2.
Presidents.] I. Title. II. Series.

E682 .K58 2002
973.8'3'092—dc21
[B]
                                                                                    2001004305
Printed in the United States of America

10 9 8 7 6 5 4 3 2 1

To Our Readers: We have done our best to make sure all Internet addresses in this book
were active and appropriate when we went to press. However, the author and the Publisher
have no control over, and assume no liability for, the material available on those Internet
sites or on other Web sites they may link to. The Publisher will try to keep the Report Links
that back up this book up to date on our Web site for three years from the book's
first publication date. Any comments or suggestions can be sent by e-mail to
comments@myreportlinks.com or to the address on the back cover.

Photo Credits: © Corel Corporation, pp. 1 (background), 3; Courtesy of
America's Library of the Library of Congress, p. 40; Courtesy of American
Memory, p. 36; Courtesy of Historical Museum of Southern Florida, p. 28;
Courtesy of Lucy Webb Hayes Photo Gallery, pp. 22, 23, 25; Courtesy of
MyReportLinks.com Books, p. 4; Courtesy of R. B. Hayes Presidential Center,
p. 33; Courtesy of Rutherford B. Hayes Presidential Center, p. 27; Courtesy of
The American President, pp. 15, 18, 38; Courtesy of The White House Web site,
pp. 12, 20; Courtesy of Ulysses S. Grant Home Page, p. 34; *Dictionary of
American Portraits*, Dover Publications, Inc., © 1967, p. 39; Library of Congress,
pp. 1, 42; Painting by Cornelia A. Fassett, 1879, p. 31.

Cover Photos: © Corel Corporation (background); White House Historical
Association.

Contents

MyReportLinks.com Books
Great Books, Great Links, Great for Research!

MyReportLinks.com Books present the information you need to learn about your report subject. In addition, they show you where to go on the Internet for more information. The pre-evaluated Report Links, listed on **www.myreportlinks.com**, save hours of research time and link to dozens—even hundreds—of Web sites, source documents, and photos related to your report topic.

To Our Readers:

Each Report Link has been reviewed by our editors, who will work hard to keep only active and appropriate Internet addresses in our books and up to date on our Web site. However, the author and the Publisher have no control over, and assume no liability for, the material available on those Internet sites, or on other Web sites they may link to.

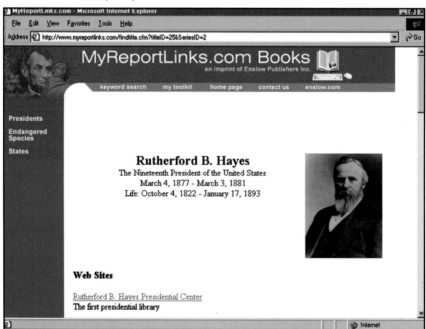

MyReportLinks.com - Microsoft Internet Explorer

File Edit View Favorites Tools Help

Address http://www.myreportlinks.com/findtitle.cfm?titleID=25&SeriesID=2 Go

MyReportLinks.com Books
an imprint of Enslow Publishers Inc.

keyword search   my toolkit   home page   contact us   enslow.com

Presidents
Endangered Species
States

Rutherford B. Hayes
The Nineteenth President of the United States
March 4, 1877 - March 3, 1881
Life: October 4, 1822 - January 17, 1893

Web Sites

Rutherford B. Hayes Presidential Center
The first presidential library

Internet

Access:

The Publisher will try to keep the Report Links that back up this book up to date on our Web site for three years from the book's first publication date. Please enter **PHA1718** if asked for a password.

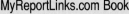
 Report Links

➤ The Internet sites described below can be accessed at
http://www.myreportlinks.com

EDITOR'S CHOICE

▶ **Rutherford B. Hayes Presidential Center**

Opened in 1916 to honor the memory of America's nineteenth
president, the Rutherford B. Hayes Library in Fremont, Ohio, was the
first presidential library in the United States. This site offers a wealth of
information about Hayes's life and presidency.

Link to this Internet site from http://www.myreportlinks.com

EDITOR'S CHOICE

▶ **Diary and Letters of Rutherford B. Hayes**

From the time he was twelve to his death at the age of seventy in 1893,
Rutherford B. Hayes kept a diary. At this site you can read these three
thousand digitalized pages of Hayes's diary.

Link to this Internet site from http://www.myreportlinks.com

EDITOR'S CHOICE

▶ **Rutherford B. Hayes: The Healer President**

This comprehensive biography of Rutherford B. Hayes provides basic
facts about Hayes, in addition to a detailed profile about his life before,
during, and after his presidency.

Link to this Internet site from http://www.myreportlinks.com

EDITOR'S CHOICE

▶ **Rutherford Birchard Hayes: 19th President of the
United States (March 4, 1877 to March 3, 1881)**

Presidents of the United States (POTUS) contains links to information
about Hayes including biographies, historical documents, election
results, and more. A great research tool.

Link to this Internet site from http://www.myreportlinks.com

EDITOR'S CHOICE

▶ **"I Do Solemnly Swear..."**

This site contains a collection of documents and images related to
Rutherford B. Hayes's inauguration. You will also find an entry from
James A. Garfield's diary regarding Hayes's Inauguration Day.

Link to this Internet site from http://www.myreportlinks.com

EDITOR'S CHOICE

▶ **Rutherford Birchard Hayes Was Born
October 4, 1822**

America's Story presents an overview of Hayes's administration. Here
you will learn how Hayes signed a bill that allowed women attorneys to
appear before the Supreme Court.

Link to this Internet site from http://www.myreportlinks.com

The Internet sites described below can be accessed at
http://www.myreportlinks.com

▶**The Twenty-third Ohio**
Rutherford B. Hayes was the third commander of the Twenty-third Ohio regiment. Here you will learn about the citizens and future presidents who volunteered to fight in the Civil War.

Link to this Internet site from http://www.myreportlinks.com

▶**The 1876 Presidential Election**
Written by Arva Moore Parks, this article describes the election of 1876 and how Florida had an impact on the outcome.

Link to this Internet site from http://www.myreportlinks.com

▶**American Presidents: Life Portraits: Rutherford B. Hayes**
This site provides "life facts" about Rutherford B. Hayes. Read Hayes's inaugural address, and learn about the key events in his administration.

Link to this Internet site from http://www.myreportlinks.com

▶**The American Presidency: Rutherford B. Hayes**
Grolier's biography of Rutherford B. Hayes covers his life from the early years, to his retirement. You will also find links to his inaugural address and quick facts about his administration.

Link to this Internet site from http://www.myreportlinks.com

▶**The American Presidency: William A. Wheeler**
William A. Wheeler served as vice president under Rutherford B. Hayes. This brief biography details Wheeler's career in politics and business.

Link to this Internet site from http://www.myreportlinks.com

▶**Booknotes Transcript**
This site holds the transcript of an interview between author Ari Hoogenboom and interviewer Brian Lamb. Here you will find interesting information about Hayes's life, presidency, and retirement.

Link to this Internet site from http://www.myreportlinks.com

Report Links

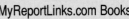

The Internet sites described below can be accessed at
http://www.myreportlinks.com

▶**Discovery School's A-to-Z History: Rutherford Birchard Hayes**
This biography contains information about Hayes's early life, political career, administration, and later years.

Link to this Internet site from http://www.myreportlinks.com

▶**Hayes vs. Tilden: The Electoral College Controversy of 1876–1877**
This site explains the electoral college controversy of 1876–1877. Here you will learn about the political situation and constitutional problems which arose from this election.

Link to this Internet site from http://www.myreportlinks.com

▶**Ohio Fundamental Documents**
From the Ohio Historical Society comes a profile of Rutherford B. Hayes's political career. Learn how Hayes was the first governor to be elected to a third term.

Link to this Internet site from http://www.myreportlinks.com

▶**Rutherford B. Hayes**
In this series, John Adams, Zachary Taylor, Jimmy Carter, and Rutherford B. Hayes are noted for having "an independent cast of mind." This site provides a brief profile of Hayes.

Link to this Internet site from http://www.myreportlinks.com

▶**Rutherford Birchard Hayes (1822–1893)**
This profile of Rutherford B. Hayes comes from ThinkQuest.org. Here you will find information about important events in the Hayes Administration, a list of his cabinet members, and his inaugural address.

Link to this Internet site from http://www.myreportlinks.com

▶**Rutherford B. Hayes (1822–1893)**
From the National Portrait Gallery comes the official portrait of Rutherford B. Hayes that hangs in the gallery in Washington D.C. This portrait was painted in 1861, more than fifteen years before he occupied the White House.

Link to this Internet site from http://www.myreportlinks.com

 The Internet sites described below can be accessed at
http://www.myreportlinks.com

▶**Rutherford B. Hayes 1822–1893**
Here you will find links to objects related to Rutherford B. Hayes. You will
also learn about the industrial development of the United States.

Link to this Internet site from http://www.myreportlinks.com

▶**Rutherford B. Hayes: Nineteenth President (1877–1881)**
This brief biography provides an overview of Rutherford B. Hayes's military
and political career.

Link to this Internet site from http://www.myreportlinks.com

▶**Rutherford B. Hayes on Grant**
This Web page contains a number of entries from the diary of Rutherford B.
Hayes about Ulysses S. Grant.

Link to this Internet site from http://www.myreportlinks.com

▶**Rutherford B. Hayes: Inaugural Address, March 5, 1877**
Bartleby.com holds the inaugural address of Rutherford B. Hayes. Because of
the controversial election of 1876, the outcome of the election was not known
until one week before the inauguration.

Link to this Internet site from http://www.myreportlinks.com

▶**Rutherford Hayes's Obituary**
By navigating through this site you will find the obituary of Rutherford B.
Hayes and a photograph of his grave site in Fremont, Ohio.

Link to this Internet site from http://www.myreportlinks.com

▶**Rutherford B. Hayes was not Such a Bad Guy**
This CNN news article discusses the similarities between the election of 1876,
between Hayes and Tilden, and the election of 2000.

Link to this Internet site from http://www.myreportlinks.com

Report Links

> The Internet sites described below can be accessed at
> **http://www.myreportlinks.com**

▶ Today in History
Here you will find information and images related to Rutherford B.
Hayes. Hayes was the first president to take the oath of office in the
Red Room of the White House.

Link to this Internet site from http://www.myreportlinks.com

▶ United States of America Chronology: The Compromise of 1877
This site provides a description of the Compromise of 1877. This
compromise brought about the withdrawal of federal troops from
the South, officially putting an end to Reconstruction.

Link to this Internet site from http://www.myreportlinks.com

▶ The White House: Lucy Ware Webb Hayes
The official White House Web site holds the biography of Lucy Ware
Webb Hayes. Well educated for a woman of her time, Lucy Ware Webb
married Rutherford B. Hayes in 1852.

Link to this Internet site from http://www.myreportlinks.com

▶ The White House: Rutherford B. Hayes
The official White House biography of Rutherford B. Hayes provides a
concise profile of Hayes's life and presidency.

Link to this Internet site from http://www.myreportlinks.com

▶ Who Won the 1876 Election?
This site provides a description of the election of 1876 and addresses
the question of who won the election and why.

Link to this Internet site from http://www.myreportlinks.com

▶ Winning the Most Popular Vote Lost the Presidency
This Web page describes three elections where the candidates with the
most popular votes did not win their elections. Here you will learn how
these elections were decided.

Link to this Internet site from http://www.myreportlinks.com

Highlights

1822—*Oct. 4:* Rutherford B. Hayes is born in Delaware, Ohio.

1842—Graduates from Kenyon College as the class valedictorian.

1845—*Jan.:* Graduates from Harvard Law School.

1852—*Dec. 30:* Marries Lucy Ware Webb in Cincinnati, Ohio.

1858–1861—Serves as Cincinnati City Solicitor.

1861–1865—Serves in the Civil War with the Twenty-third Ohio Volunteer Infantry Regiment.

1861—*Oct. 24:* Promoted to lieutenant colonel.

1862—*Sep. 14:* Left arm is wounded at Battle of South Mountain.

—*Oct. 24:* Promoted to colonel.

1864—*Oct. 9:* Promoted to brigadier general of volunteers.

1865—*March 3:* Promoted to brevetted major general of volunteers.

—*June 8:* Resigns from the Army.

1865–1867—Serves as a congressman in the U.S. House of Representatives.

1867—Elected governor of Ohio; serves 1867–72, and later from 1876–77.

1876—Elected nineteenth president of the United States over Samuel J. Tilden. William Almon Wheeler is elected vice president.

1877—Withdraws the last Union soldiers from the South, thus ending Reconstruction.

1878—*Oct. 4:* First Chinese embassy officials are received by the Hayes Administration.

1880—*March:* Hayes is first president to formulate a policy regarding building a canal across Panama under American control.

1893—*Jan. 17:* Dies in Fremont, Ohio, of a heart attack.

Struggle for Survival, September 1862

The United States had fallen apart. The Civil War between the North and South had broken out. Many of the southern states had seceded, or broken free from the United States and formed the Confederate States of America.

Thousands of men rushed to enlist on both sides. One of them was Rutherford B. Hayes. He became a lieutenant colonel in the United States army.

On September 14, 1862, Hayes was part of the Union force trying to break through Fox's Gap in the Blue Ridge Mountains, in southern Maryland. Ahead of them were dozens of Confederate troops (also called Rebels) dug in behind trees and fences. Getting through the gap would be a difficult, bloody task.

"When we charge, yell!" Hayes told his men. "Scare the rebels. Make it sound like thousands are attacking." Then he yelled, "Give them hell!"[1] Together they hollered and charged through the woods up the hill.

Soon clouds of smoke wafted through the trees. Muskets fired. Cannons boomed. Screams echoed up and down the hill as soldiers on both sides were wounded and killed. This became known as the Battle of South Mountain.

"The enemy broke," Hayes remembered, "and we drove them clear out of the woods."[2] His men dove behind fences and continued their fire. The Rebels huddled behind stonewalls higher up the hill.

After a few moments, Hayes decided it was time to start moving again. Just then he was shot. A musket ball

caught him above the left elbow. His arm was broken. Blood covered his uniform. "I soon felt weak, faint, and sick at the stomach."[3] One of his men tied a handkerchief around the wound.

From the ground Hayes watched the battle. "The enemy's fire was occasionally very heavy; balls passed near my face and hit the ground all around me. I could see wounded men staggering or carried to the rear."[4]

When some of his men took a few steps back into the woods, he struggled back to his feet and ordered them to hold their positions.

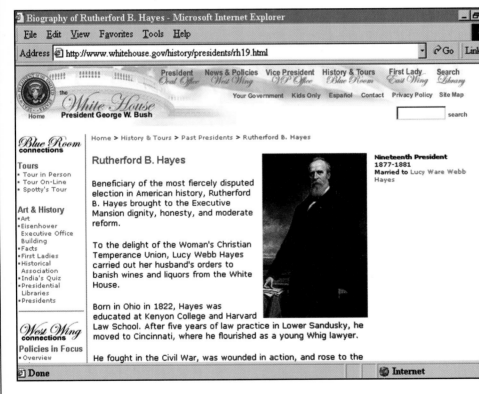

A Civil War hero, Hayes never hesitated to show courage and bravery on the battlefield. His presidential task of putting the war-torn country back together would prove to be a difficult one.

A tired, scared sergeant begged, "I am played out; please sir, let me leave."

Hayes became angry. He used his sword to point to his bloody arm. "Look at this," he shouted. "Don't talk about being played out. There is your place in line."[5] The sergeant returned to the battle, and Hayes soon collapsed from his wound.

As the fighting continued, the colonel struck up a conversation with a wounded Rebel soldier, who was also on the ground a few feet away. "You came a good ways to fight us," Hayes told him.[6] "We were right jolly and friendly."[7]

Hayes had no way of knowing how seriously he was wounded. He thought there was a chance he would die on the battlefield. "I gave him [the Rebel soldier] messages for my wife and friends in case I should not get up."[8]

Hayes eventually got up. He had survived the fight and was helped off the battlefield. Later that day the Union troops finally pushed the Confederate Army out of the gap.

In less than fifteen years after he lay wounded on the battlefield, Rutherford B. Hayes would become president of the United States. His most important job in the White House, he decided, was to finish putting the country back together.

Chapter 2 ▶

Formative Years, 1822–1845

Rutherford Birchard Hayes was named after his father, although he never met the man. Rutherford Hayes, Jr., the president's father, grew up in Vermont. Rutherford Birchard's grandfather ran a tavern in Brattleboro, Vermont, and his father managed a store in nearby Dummerston. It was there that Rutherford Hayes, Jr., met and married Sophia Birchard. It was there, too, that their first son, Lorenzo, was born. After the War of 1812, times were tough in Vermont. People did not have much money and business at the store was poor. Hayes decided life would be better if he moved west.

In the early nineteenth century, Ohio was on the edge of the frontier. It was not even a state yet. Rutherford and Sophia moved there with Lorenzo in 1817. Their daughter, Fanny, was born in Ohio in 1820.

▶ The Man of the House

Unfortunately, the young father was struck with a fever and died when Fanny was still a baby. His widow, Sophia, was pregnant. Ten weeks after his father's death, Rutherford Birchard Hayes, was born on October 4, 1822, in Delaware, Ohio.

The family was not well off. When young Rutherford was about a year old, they moved into a new house in Delaware, but did not even have enough money to buy new furniture. The other families in the neighborhood had plenty of picture books for their children. Not Lorenzo, Fanny, and Rutherford. Mrs. Hayes could not afford them.

▲ *Hayes named his daughter Fanny in honor of his sister.*

Lorenzo seemed to be a proud big brother. "He was kind and good-natured, prompt, energetic, and courageous, and the earliest protector of his little sister,"[1] related Rutherford. But in January 1825, nine-year-old Lorenzo laced on his ice skates and headed for a millpond in Delaware. He fell through the ice and drowned. Two-year-old Rutherford, a frail boy with red hair and blue eyes, was now the man of the house.

Farm Life

The shock of losing her husband and her oldest son made Sophia Hayes a very protective mother. Because

Rutherford always seemed to be sick, she almost never allowed him to go outside to play. When Rutherford was little, Mrs. Hayes did not even let him go to school. She taught him herself.

Even though she, too, was still a youngster, Fanny took special care of Rutherford. Sometimes Mrs. Hayes would let Fanny bring her little brother outside to play. Rutherford's earliest memories are of his sister taking him "carefully about the garden and barnyard and on short visits to the nearest neighbors. She was loving and kind to me and very generous."[2]

The Hayes family loved visiting the farm they owned about ten miles from their home. Sometimes they rode there on horseback, but usually they walked. Hayes remembered, "Sugar-making, cider-making, cherry time, and gathering hickory nuts and walnuts were the occasions of these . . . delightful trips."[3]

When Rutherford was five, Fanny almost died from dysentery, a serious intestinal disease. It became her brother's turn to take care of her. "After she was able to sit up, I daily gave her little rides upon a small hand-sled which with great difficulty I hauled about the garden. We were both very happy."[4]

▶ School Years

Finally, Mrs. Hayes allowed both her children to leave the house and go to school together. Her brother, Sardis, a successful businessman, had become the children's guardian. Money was no longer a problem. Rutherford and Fanny had all the books they wanted.

School then was very different than it is today. The classroom was crowded with children of all ages, even a few young adults. Hayes later remembered his teacher,

Daniel Granger, as "a little, thin, wiry, energetic Yankee with . . . piercing black eyes."[5] The teacher was "a demon of ferocity" who was not afraid of paddling his students. "He flogged great strapping fellows of twice his size, and talked savagely of . . . throwing them through the walls of the schoolhouse."[6]

Once a boy sitting next to Rutherford dared to whisper during class. Granger threw a large jack-knife at the boy's head. It just missed. "All the younger scholars were horribly afraid of him. We thought our lives were in danger. We knew he would kill some of us."[7] Still, Rutherford survived the class and became a fine speller. He later bragged that nobody could spell better than he did.

A Vermont Adventure

In 1834, when Rutherford was twelve, Sophia Hayes took her children back to Vermont to meet their relatives. It was a long trip by stagecoach, steamboat, train, and canal boat. Rutherford kept a journal of the trip in his notebook.

In the journal, his spelling was good, but he did not bother to use much punctuation. He listed all the relatives and towns they visited, but he also wrote about the adventures he had. "I had lots of fun with George breaking up bumblebees' nests."[8]

After church in Brattleboro, the Hayes children and a friend walked down to a river. "We sent Fanny in after sticks. We then put a board across the brook; we then climbed up the rocks and went down to where the river run in a very narrow place."[9]

Fanny's Influence

Back in Ohio, Rutherford and Fanny spent most of their time together. "Fanny was in the habit of teasing me a great deal," he said. "To her ridicule I could only oppose my superior strength . . . We had many little quarrels, she always having the better with her tongue and I with my fists . . . We loved each other dearly and yet behaved often as if we were hateful."[10]

Since Uncle Sardis, his guardian, was a wealthy man, Rutherford would be one of the few lucky boys from Delaware to attend college. It would take more than Granger's lessons at the local school to prepare him, though. When he was fourteen, he moved to Norwalk, Ohio, where he attended the Methodist Academy. Then he transferred to a private school in Middletown, Connecticut.

gal 1 - Microsoft Internet Explorer

File   Edit   View   Favorites   Tools   Help

Address http://www.americanpresident.org/KoTrain/courses/RBH/gal_1.htm   Go   Links

[Return to Bio]

Internet

▲ *Rutherford B. Hayes at the age of twenty-four.*

Rutherford continued to encounter memorable teachers. "The French tutor," he wrote, "is a passionate old fellow. He looks more like a plump feather bed than anything else I know of."[11]

By 1838, he was ready for Kenyon College in Gambier, Ohio. Sometimes his writing was more serious. "I am willing to study hard," he promised. He wanted to grow to be a "true friend and good citizen. To become such a man I shall necessarily have to live in accordance with the precepts of the Bible."[12] After four years at Kenyon, Rutherford graduated at the top of his class. Then, probably to please Fanny, he decided to be a lawyer.

Hayes was a fine enough student to earn acceptance to Harvard College, in Cambridge, Massachusetts. He graduated from Harvard Law School in 1845.

Hayes left Massachusetts for Lower Sandusky (later Fremont), Ohio, the hometown of his Uncle Sardis. There he began his career as a lawyer.

Chapter 3 ▶

New Ambitions, 1850–1876

Rutherford B. Hayes spent five quiet years in Fremont, but he was too ambitious to stay there for long. It was too quiet, and there was very little legal business. In 1850 he moved to Cincinnati, Ohio's biggest city.

At first, things in Cincinnati were just as quiet as they had been for him in Fremont. He had so few clients that

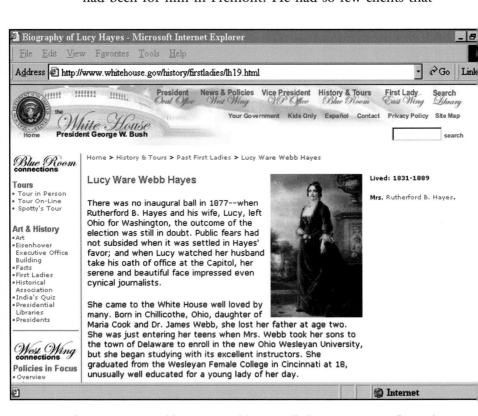

Biography of Lucy Hayes - Microsoft Internet Explorer

File   Edit   View   Favorites   Tools   Help

Address http://www.whitehouse.gov/history/firstladies/lh19.html   Go   Link

President   News & Policies   Vice President   History & Tours   First Lady   Search
Oval Office   West Wing   VP Office   Blue Room   East Wing   Library

the White House   Your Government   Kids Only   Español   Contact   Privacy Policy   Site Map
Home   President George W. Bush   search

Blue Room connections

Home > History & Tours > Past First Ladies > Lucy Ware Webb Hayes

Tours
• Tour in Person
• Tour On-Line
• Spotty's Tour

Lucy Ware Webb Hayes

Lived: 1831-1889

Mrs. Rutherford B. Hayes.

Art & History
• Art
• Eisenhower Executive Office Building
• Facts
• First Ladies
• Historical Association
• India's Quiz
• Presidential Libraries
• Presidents

There was no inaugural ball in 1877--when Rutherford B. Hayes and his wife, Lucy, left Ohio for Washington, the outcome of the election was still in doubt. Public fears had not subsided when it was settled in Hayes' favor; and when Lucy watched her husband take his oath of office at the Capitol, her serene and beautiful face impressed even cynical journalists.

She came to the White House well loved by many. Born in Chillicothe, Ohio, daughter of Maria Cook and Dr. James Webb, she lost her father at age two. She was just entering her teens when Mrs. Webb took her sons to the town of Delaware to enroll in the new Ohio Wesleyan University, but she began studying with its excellent instructors. She graduated from the Wesleyan Female College in Cincinnati at 18, unusually well educated for a young lady of her day.

West Wing connections

Policies in Focus
• Overview

Internet

▲ *Lucy Ware Webb Hayes would eventually become a very influential and powerful first lady.*

he did not make enough money to rent an apartment. He had to sleep in his office.

Then, slowly, Hayes's business picked up. Word got out that he was a talented attorney. In 1852, he was the defense lawyer in two widely-publicized murder trials. His strong arguments saved both defendants from the death penalty.

▶ Lucy Webb

Hayes had more on his mind than legal arguments. Five years before, he had attended a meeting in Delaware with his mother and sister. There he had met Lucy Webb, a pretty fifteen-year-old. Hayes told friends she was "a bright sunny hearted little girl not quite old enough to fall in love with—and so I didn't."[1]

Mrs. Hayes, however, decided that Lucy would be a perfect wife for her son, even though he was almost nine years older. Hayes joked, "Mother . . . selected a clever little school-girl named Webb for me in Delaware."[2]

Lucy Webb was more than just clever. Even though most women did not even finish high school, Lucy graduated and then enrolled at the Cincinnati Wesleyan Female College. She was a student there when Hayes moved his law practice to the same city.

Soon after moving to Cincinnati, the young lawyer visited Lucy at college. Shortly after, he wrote in his diary about "the bright eyes and merry smile of the lovely girl whose image is so often in my thoughts."[3] Besides her beauty, Hayes wrote about her intelligence and kindness.

When Lucy discovered a family that needed help because the father was ill, she collected food, clothing, medicine, and wood for them. "Blessed angel," Hayes wrote, "I loved her doubly for it."[4]

▲ *Hayes was wildly in love with his wife Lucy when they married on December 30, 1852. He expressed his love for her in the many journals he wrote throughout his life.*

The Hayes family enjoyed the growing romance, but thought it was moving too slowly. Finally Uncle Sardis asked, "Why doesn't the fool marry her?"[5]

The wedding was eventually held on December 30, 1852. Lucy wore a floor-length veil, covered with orange blossoms. After the ceremony, the couple got on a train for Columbus, Ohio. Several hours of their honeymoon were spent in the Supreme Court chamber, where Hayes was arguing a case.

Rutherford Hayes was wildly in love. "A better wife I never hoped to have," he wrote. "Blessings on his head who first invented marriage."[6]

On November 4, 1853, their first child, a son named Sardis Birchard Hayes, was born. Rutherford and Lucy were overjoyed. "When I take him in my arms, I begin to feel a father's love and interest, hope and pride," Hayes wrote. But as always his thoughts returned to wife. "How I love Lucy, the mother of my boy!"[7]

Over the next sixteen years, Mrs. Hayes would give birth to seven more children. Three boys died when they were still babies. The other children were sons: Webb, Rutherford, Scott, and a daughter named Fanny.

lwhbaby - Microsoft Internet Explorer

File Edit View Favorites Tools Help

Address http://www.rbhayes.org/lwh_images/pages/lwhbaby.htm   Go Links

Internet

▲ Lucy Hayes holds the couple's oldest son Birchard Austin Hayes, the source of his father's "love and interest, hope and pride."

▶ A Growing Career

As his family grew, so did his law practice. In 1858, the Cincinnati City Council appointed him city solicitor. Because of his opposition to slavery, Hayes offered free legal services to runaway slaves and other whites and African Americans, who helped runaway slaves. His views about slavery also led him to join the new Republican Party, which was strongly opposed to the spread of slavery.

Not all Americans supported the new party. Southern slave owners wanted to be left alone. When Abraham Lincoln, the Republican candidate, was elected president in 1860, the southern states left the Union and established the Confederate States of America. Soon the differences between the two regions exploded into the bloody Civil War.

▶ "A Just and Necessary War"

"This was a just and necessary war," Hayes decided. "I would prefer to go into it if I knew I was to die or be killed in the course of it, than to live through and after it without taking any part in it."[8]

Following his ideals, Rutherford B. Hayes left his wife, children, job, and his home to fight for the Union cause. He was appointed a major and served bravely for four years. His regiment fought in many battles. Four times his horse was shot out from under him; five times he himself was wounded.

While the war raged, Hayes was nominated for the U.S. House of Representatives. Some members of his party expected him to leave the Army so that he could campaign back home. The suggestion made Hayes angry. "An officer . . . who at this crisis would abandon his post to electioneer for a seat in Congress ought to be scalped," he wrote. "You

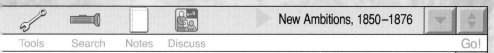

lwhwound - Microsoft Internet Explorer

File　Edit　View　Favorites　Tools　Help

Address　http://www.rbhayes.org/lwh_images/pages/lwhwound.htm　　Go　Links »

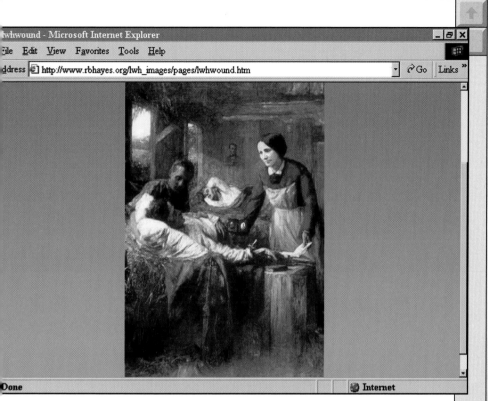

Done　　　　　　　　　　　　　　　　Internet

Lucy Hayes shared and supported her husband's interest in the Civil War. While Hayes was away fighting for the Union cause, she visited wounded soldiers and helped care for them.

may feel perfectly sure I shall do no such thing."[9] Hayes won the election, but he never left his regiment to serve in Washington. When the war ended with a Union victory in 1865, he was a brevet major general. Finally, he was willing to resign to return to his family in Ohio, and then to his new position in Washington, D.C. While in the Army, Hayes grew a beard, which he would keep for the rest of his life.

Entering Politics

While in the House of Representatives, Hayes earned praise for his work as chairman of the Joint Committee on

the Library of Congress. He was popular enough that the people of his district re-elected him in 1866.

The popular war hero did not spend much time in Congress. Republicans thought he would make a great candidate for governor. As a result, he resigned from Congress, left Washington, and returned to campaign in Ohio.

Hayes championed the cause of suffrage (the right to vote) for African Americans, an unpopular stand even in a northern state, but he still won the election. As governor, he pushed the Fifteenth Amendment through the Ohio legislature. The amendment was designed to guarantee the right to vote to African Americans across the nation. Governor Hayes devoted much attention to reforming Ohio's schools, prisons, and mental hospitals. He helped establish the college that would become Ohio State University.

When his second term ended, he planned to retire permanently from politics, but Republican leaders persuaded him to run again for Congress. This time he lost and returned to Fremont. His Uncle Sardis had died, leaving him Spiegel Grove, a large estate, and a fair amount of money. Hayes spent three years expanding his personal fortune with a real estate business.

▶ Governor Once Again

In 1875, the Republican Party needed a strong candidate to run against the popular Democrat William Allen for governor of Ohio. Allen, known as a "Greenback," wanted the government to improve the economy by printing more paper, or "green," money. Hayes thought that would be irresponsible. He was in favor of a "sound-money policy," which limited the amount of money printed by the government.

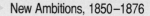

Address http://www.rbhayes.org/home.htm

Done   Internet

When his Uncle Sardis died, Hayes acquired the property called *Spiegel Grove*. It is now the site of the Hayes family home, a thirty-three room mansion, as well as a library, museum, and tomb.

Hayes won the election and went back to work in Columbus. He captured national attention by cutting the state budget. He also supported a strong civil service program, which awarded state jobs to the most qualified applicants. In the past, many had gotten jobs simply because they were in the same party as the governor who was in power.

In 1876, President Ulysses S. Grant was finishing his second term and refusing to run again. The Republican Party needed a candidate. The popular, honest, reform-minded, hard-working governor of Ohio seemed a possible choice to some voters.

Disputed Election, 1876–1877

The presidential election of 1876 was one of the strangest in American history. It was a time of widespread corruption. Many government officials, including some of President Ulysses S. Grant's closest advisors, were caught taking bribes. It seemed to many voters that public officials were more interested in getting rich than in doing their jobs.

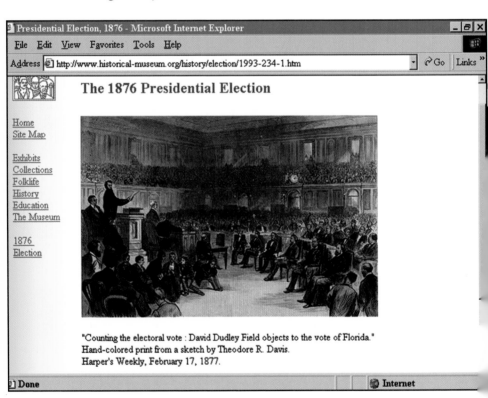

Presidential Election, 1876 - Microsoft Internet Explorer

File Edit View Favorites Tools Help

Address http://www.historical-museum.org/history/election/1993-234-1.htm   Go   Links »

Home
Site Map

Exhibits
Collections
Folklife
History
Education
The Museum

1876
Election

The 1876 Presidential Election

"Counting the electoral vote : David Dudley Field objects to the vote of Florida."
Hand-colored print from a sketch by Theodore R. Davis.
Harper's Weekly, February 17, 1877.

Done   Internet

▲ The election of 1876 was one of the strangest presidential elections in history, with three Southern states having disputed results. This sketch shows the counting of the electoral vote.

A Clean Record

To win over voters bothered by the scandals, the Democrats nominated Samuel J. Tilden. He had fought hard against government corruption as governor of New York.

James G. Blaine, a former speaker of the House, and Senator Roscoe Conkling, both wanted the Republican nomination, but neither could get enough votes at the convention. The delegates finally decided on Rutherford B. Hayes. He was a war hero with a clean record. Republicans figured he had a good chance against Tilden.

Reconstruction

One of the biggest issues facing the nation in 1876 was Reconstruction. After the Civil War had ended, Congress decided not to simply let the southern states back into the Union. The Army was temporarily put in charge of those areas. Southerners had to promise to allow former slaves a voice in the government. New state constitutions had to be written. Then the states would be allowed, one by one, to reenter the Union.

Many white Southerners resented Reconstruction. They did not like the presence of army troops or the new constitutions. They were upset by Northerners having influence over the South. Mostly, they opposed giving black men the right to vote. Southern whites felt Reconstruction was being unfairly imposed on them. Most Democrats, in both the North and South, sympathized with the Southern whites.

Republicans, on the other hand, supported rights for African Americans. They blamed the South for the Civil War and felt whites there should pay a price for tearing the country apart.

While he was a congressman, Hayes had strongly supported Reconstruction. He had felt it was the only way to insure the participation of African Americans in government. Most voters believed that if he became president, Hayes would continue to back Reconstruction.

▶ A Controversial Election

The election campaign of 1876 was a quiet affair. Hayes rarely left Ohio. When he asked his vice presidential candidate, William A. Wheeler, to make a few speeches, Hayes got a strange reply. "Speaking, and the presence of crowds, excite me and intensify my wakefulness," Wheeler said.[1] Since giving speeches caused Wheeler to worry and to lose sleep, he kept quiet.

On election night, Hayes went to bed believing he had lost. Tilden had received 4,284,020 votes to 4,036,572 for Hayes. That gave the Democrats a majority of almost 250,000 popular votes. A headline in the *New York Tribune* declared, "Tilden Elected."[2]

Hayes did not seem upset. In a letter written the day after the election, he said his young son Scott was happy. Now he would not have to move to Washington and could stay with his friends in Columbus.

The election was not over yet. Then, as now, people seem to forget that presidents are not elected by popular votes. Presidential elections are decided by electoral votes. According to the U.S. Constitution, states are assigned electoral votes based on their population. States with more people have more votes. In 1876, there were 369 electoral votes divided among the thirty-seven states. To win, a candidate had to get a majority, or at least 185.

Zachariah Chandler, the Republican National Chairman, surveyed the results and announced, "Hayes

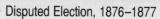
has 185 votes and is elected."[3] Democrats were outraged. According to their figures, Tilden had beaten Hayes, 204 to 165.

The problem was that three Southern states—Louisiana, Florida, and South Carolina—had disputed results. Republicans claimed to have more votes in all three states. Democrats believed they had won.

When the undisputed electoral votes were counted, Tilden led Hayes, 184–165. The Democrat was ahead, but he was one vote short of winning. That meant he needed just one of the twenty disputed votes to win. Hayes needed them all.

Congress appointed a commission to decide the matter. If the commission could not reach a decision, the House of Representatives would get to choose the new president.

▲ In this painting, artist Cornelia B. Fasset depicts the electoral commission that decided the election of 1876.

Since the House had a Democratic majority, it would pick Tilden.

Republicans correctly argued that southern white Democrats had cheated by denying African Americans the right to vote. The Republicans felt most African Americans would vote for the Republican candidate, thus allowing them to win those states. Democrats claimed that despite the African-American vote, they had taken all three of the disputed states. Many African Americans had in fact been prevented from voting by fraud, violence, or threats that they might be killed if they tried to vote.

The argument continued for weeks. Each party accused the other of trying to steal the election. There was talk by radicals in both parties of taking the White House by force.

In Ohio, Hayes's children worried about their father's safety. During dinner at their home one evening, a bullet was fired through a window. Little Scott pretended to read his older sister a story, "R. B. Hayes is elected, and the Democrats will kill him . . . And they will kill all the Republicans."[4] Scott's older brother, Webb, carried a pistol and accompanied his father whenever he left the house.

▶ A Deal is Made

Then came a compromise. Republicans promised that if Hayes were named president, he would withdraw all remaining federal troops in the southern states. At least one southern Democrat would be named to the president's Cabinet. Money would be set aside for the rebuilding of railroad tracks and other improvements in the South. Reconstruction would be over. The southern states would be free to run their states as they saw fit. There was some grumbling, but the Democrats finally accepted the deal.

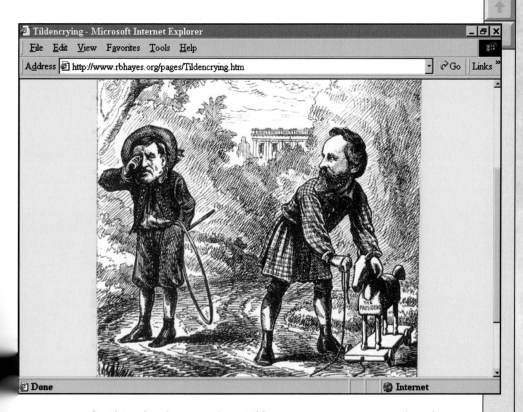

▲ *This political cartoon shows Tilden crying as Hayes assumes his role as president.*

Republicans were surprised and happy that they had prevailed. Hayes believed the promises his party made would help bring the country back together. Instead of being forced by federal troops to follow the law, Southerners would be free to decide what was right. Hayes was convinced that they would be fair to the former slaves. The war had been over for eleven years; it was time to treat the South the same way that every other region of America was treated. Unfortunately, Hayes was wrong, and the end of Reconstruction led to segregation and the denial of rights for African Americans throughout the South.

When the Hayes family left Columbus for Washington, the commission had yet to announce its decision. Nobody knew who had won. Early in the morning on March 2, a telegram was rushed aboard Hayes's train in Harrisburg, Pennsylvania. The news was good; he had been elected. His friends and advisors began cheering. "Boys, boys," the president-elect told them, "you'll waken the passengers."[5]

▲ Ulysses S. Grant was one of Hayes's closest friends. In one of his journal entries Hayes wrote, "We had a quiet nice time last night. A most agreeable talk with General Grant for two hours alone. He looks well and is in excellent spirits."

▶ The Secret Inauguration

According to the Constitution, the new president was supposed to take office on March 4. Since that day fell on a Sunday in 1877, the inauguration ceremony was postponed until the following day.

Republican President Ulysses S. Grant had a different idea—and a secret plan. He did not trust the Democrats; he was afraid they would not keep their part of the election deal. Grant did not want Hayes to wait to be sworn in.

Therefore, on the evening of March 4, Grant invited the Hayes family and thirty-eight other guests to the White House for dinner. The guests gathered in the East Room, then walked as a group to the dining room. Nobody noticed that Grant and Hayes slipped away. Just as nobody had noticed when Chief Justice Morrison R. Waite slipped into the White House a few moments before. He was waiting in the Red Room.

It did not take long for Waite to administer the oath of office to Hayes. When the men joined the rest of the guests in the dining room, Rutherford B. Hayes was the president of the United States.

A Loyal American, 1877–1880

At his official inauguration ceremony on March 5, 1877, President Rutherford B. Hayes had a simple message. "He serves his party best who serves the country best."[1]

Hayes was a loyal Republican, but he wanted people in both parties to know that he was going to do what was

American Memory Digital Item Display - 00650939 - Microsoft Internet Explorer

File Edit View Favorites Tools Help

Address pin:@field(NUMBER+@band(ppmsc+02923)):displayType=1:m856sd=ppmsc:m856sf=02923 Go Link

Done — Internet

▲ At his inaugural ceremony pictured here, Hayes delivered a simple, yet comforting message; "He serves his party best who serves his country best." He wanted to show Americans that he would act in the best interest of the country.

right for the country. Some Democrats did not believe the new president meant what he said.

His first order of business was to issue an executive order banning political activity by federal office holders. He wanted government workers to be busy at their jobs, not campaigning. Two friends of Republican Senator Roscoe Conkling did not think the new rule applied to them. Even though they were supposed to be working for the government in New York City, Chester A. Arthur and Alonzo B. Cornell stayed busy in political affairs. Hayes did not hesitate. He removed both men from their jobs. That action, as it turned out, did not hurt the political career of either man. Cornell was later elected governor of New York. Arthur became president.

Even still, Hayes's action showed that he was serious about workers doing their jobs. It was one of the first steps taken to separate national civil service jobs from political considerations.

The careful financial policies of the Hayes administration helped the nation recover from a depression. Business improved and thousands of jobs were created.

Campaigning for Equality

President Hayes paid serious attention to the problems of African Americans. He stopped Congress from passing laws that would have made it easier to keep African Americans from voting. When Johnson C. Whittaker, an African-American cadet, was unfairly dismissed from the West Point Military Academy, Hayes reinstated him and fired the academy's superintendent. He also appointed Frederick Douglass, the nation's most famous African-American man, U.S. Marshal for the District of Columbia.

▲ *The Hayes family.*

Despite his hopes, the status of African Americans worsened in the South. Hayes kept his party's promises and Reconstruction ended. Without troops, he had to rely on the good will of Southerners to be fair to African Americans. That did not happen. Despite the Fifteenth Amendment, soon African Americans in the South lost the right to vote. Discrimination against them became law.

▶ Life at the White House

Three of the Hayes children lived in the White House with their parents. Ten-year-old Fanny kept her doll houses in an upstairs hallway. She and her younger brother Scott were tutored in the mansion. Webb, his father's secretary, was with the president almost all the time. Since he still carried a pistol, he also served as a bodyguard.

Lucy Hayes was the first president's wife to have been a college graduate. She was also probably the first to be known as the First Lady. Mrs. Hayes was also a firm believer in temperance—the campaign against alcoholic beverages such as whiskey or beer. She refused to allow alcohol to be served at dinners or parties at the White House. People who missed the booze later gave her the nickname Lemonade Lucy. Mr. and Mrs. Hayes also started the tradition of the "Easter Egg Roll" for children on the White House lawn. It continues today each year on the Monday after Easter.

In 1880, the British government sent Hayes a unique gift. It was a beautiful desk made from the timbers of *HMS Resolute*, a ship that had been abandoned in the Arctic. The president displayed the big desk in the Green Room before moving it upstairs to his private office. After he left the White House, it was put in storage.

Eighty years later, in 1961, President John F. Kennedy discovered the desk and moved it into the Oval Office. It has been used by presidents ever since.

New Advances

Technology was changing the way Americans lived in

"Lemonade Lucy" was a very powerful first lady. She supported many of the leading moral causes of the day, namely the abolition of slavery, prohibition of alcohol, and aid to the poor.

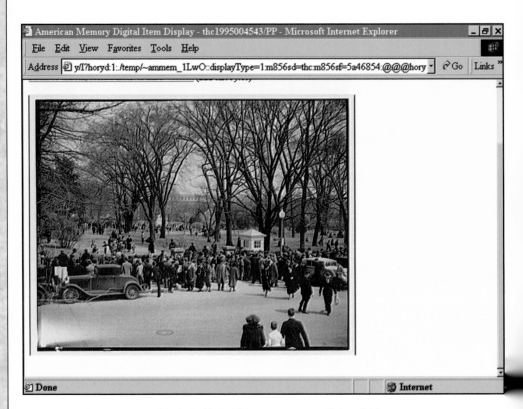

American Memory Digital Item Display - thc1995004543/PP - Microsoft Internet Explorer

File   Edit   View   Favorites   Tools   Help

Address y/I7horyd:1:./temp/~ammem_1LwO::displayType=1:m856sd=thc:m856sf=5a46854:@@@hory   Go   Links

Done   Internet

The Hayes family held the first Easter Egg Roll for children. Here is a photo taken in 1936 of later generations continuing the annual tradition.

the 1870s. The transcontinental railroad had been completed in 1869. Now railways linked the nation from coast to coast. Hayes became the first president to ride the transcontinental railroad when he traveled to the West Coast during his presidency.

Shortly after he was inaugurated, Hayes talked on a telephone with Alexander Graham Bell. Soon a phone was installed in the White House telegraph room. However, it was not of much use since hardly any other offices had one.

Ever since the time of George Washington's administration, official papers had been written out in longhand. But Hayes ordered a new invention called a typewriter.

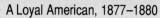

Soon his secretaries were using the keyboards and ink ribbons to print letters and orders.

One-Term President

Rutherford Hayes never made a secret of the fact that he intended only to serve one term as president. He probably would not have been re-nominated by his party if he had wanted to run. Many Republicans were not happy with his attempts to reform civil service. There were also those who thought he had done too much to help African Americans. Others did not think he had done enough.

Chapter 6

Campaigner Until the End, 1891–1893

After a long convention in 1880, Hayes was pleased when the Republicans nominated his friend, James A. Garfield. Unlike Hayes, Garfield defeated his Democratic opponent, Winfield S. Hancock, both in the electoral total (214 to 155) and in the popular vote (by just 9,644).

Hayes was relieved. In a letter to his friend, Guy Bryan, he wrote, "Nobody ever left the presidency with less regret, less disappointment, fewer heartburnings, or more general content with the result of his term (in his own heart, I mean) than I do."[1]

After attending Garfield's inauguration ceremony, Hayes boarded a train headed for Ohio. The train collided with another just outside of Baltimore. Two people were killed and twenty were seriously hurt in the crash. Hayes, however, was thrown from his chair but unhurt.

The Hayes family went home to Fremont, Ohio, where they lived in Spiegel Grove, the mansion built by Hayes's uncle, Sardis Birchard. The former president had nothing more to do with politics. Instead, he promoted causes such as prison reform and public education. For a time, he was president of the National Prison Association.

◀ *After his term as president, Hayes retired to Spiegel Grove, where he died in 1893.*

He was especially interested in the growth of Ohio State University. He served on boards that distributed scholarships to needy students, both black and white. Among them were the George Peabody Educational Fund and the John F. Slater Fund. He also participated in the Lake Mohonk Conferences, which promoted the advancement of African Americans and American Indians.

Lucy Hayes died in 1889. Four years later, her husband had an attack of angina in Cleveland. His friends wanted him to rest, but he insisted on returning home. "I would rather die at Spiegel Grove," he said, "than to live anywhere else."[2] Rutherford B. Hayes died of a heart attack in his own bed on January 17, 1893.

Chapter 1. Struggle for Survival, September 1862

1. T. Harry Williams, *Hayes of the Twenty-Third* (Lincoln: University of Nebraska Press, 1965), p. 137.

2. Rutherford B. Hayes, *The Diary and Letters of Rutherford B. Hayes: Nineteenth President of the United States* (Columbus, Ohio: Ohio State Archeological and Historical Society, 1922), pp. 355–356; published on *Ohio History*, n.d., <http://www.ohiohistory.org/onlinedoc/hayes/chapterxx.html> (June 20, 2001).

3. Ibid., p. 356.

4. Ibid.

5. Williams, p. 138.

6. Ibid.

7. Hayes, p. 357.

8. Ibid.

Chapter 2. Formative Years, 1822–1845

1. Rutherford B. Hayes, *The Diary and Letters of Rutherford B. Hayes: Nineteenth President of the United States* (Columbus, Ohio: Ohio State Archeological and Historical Society, 1922), p. 4; published on *Ohio History*, n.d., <http://www.ohiohistory.org/onlinedoc/hayes/chapterxx.html> (June 20, 2001).

2. Ibid.

3. Ibid., p. 6.

4. Ibid., p. 9.

5. Ibid.

6. Ibid.

7. Ibid., p. 1.

8. Ibid., pp. 2–3.

9. Ibid., p. 11.

10. "Memorable Quotes from the Diary and Letters of Rutherford B. Hayes," *Ohio History*, n.d., <http://www.ohiohistory.org/onlinedoc/hayes/quotes.html> (June 20, 2001).

11. Ibid.

12. Ibid.

Chapter 3. New Ambitions, 1850–1876

1. Emily Apt Geer, *First Lady: The Life of Lucy Webb Hayes* (Fremont, Ohio: Rutherford B. Hayes Presidential Center, 1995), p. 7.

2. Ibid., pp. 7–8.

3. Ibid., p. 18.

4. Ibid., p. 21.

5. Ibid., p. 23.

6. Ibid., p. 28.

7. "Memorable Quotes from the Diary and Letters of Rutherford B. Hayes," *Ohio History*, n.d., <http://www.ohiohistory.org/onlinedoc/hayes/quotes.html> (June 20, 2001).

8. Ibid.

9. Ibid.

Chapter 4. Disputed Election, 1876–1877

1. Donald A. Ritchie, "1876." In *Running for President: The Candidates and Their Images 1789–1896* edited by Arthur M. Schlesinger, Jr., et. al., (New York: Simon & Schuster, 1994), p. 327.

2. Ibid., p. 329.

3. "Rutherford B. Hayes: Nineteenth President 1877–1881," *Presidents*, n.d., <http://www.whitehouse.gov/history/presidents/rh19.html> (June 20, 2001).

4. Emily Apt Geer, *First Lady: The Life of Lucy Webb Hayes* (Fremont, Ohio: Rutherford B. Hayes Presidential Center, 1995), p. 129.

5. William Seale, *The President's House: A History* (Washington, D.C.: White House Historical Association, 1986), p. 488.

Chapter 5. A Loyal American, 1877–1880

1. Rutherford B. Hayes, "Inaugural Address Given at Capitol Building, Washington, DC: Monday, March 5, 1877," *History Buff: Rutherford B. Hayes's Inaugural Address*-Discovery.com, n.d., <http://www.discovery.com/guides/history/historybuff/presidents/hayes.html> (June 21, 2001).

Chapter 6. Campaigner Until the End, 1881–1893

1. Rutherford B. Hayes, *The Diary and Letters of Rutherford B. Hayes: Nineteenth President of the United States* (Columbus, Ohio: Ohio State Archeological and Historical Society, 1922), p. 632; published on *Ohio History*, n.d., <http://www.ohiohistory.org/onlinedoc/hayes/chapterxxxviii.html> (June 21, 2001).

2. Rutherford B. Hayes, *The Diary and Letters of Rutherford B. Hayes: Nineteenth President of the United States* (Columbus, Ohio: Ohio State Archeological and Historical Society, 1922), Appendix D, p. 318; published on *Ohio History*, n.d., <http://www.ohiohistory.org/onlinedoc/hayes/appendixd.html> (June 21, 2001).

Green, Carl R. and William R. Sanford. *Union Generals of the Civil War.* Springfield, N.J.: Enslow Publishers, Inc., 1998.

Greer, Emily A. *First Lady: The Life of Lucy Webb Hayes.* Kent, Ohio: Kent State University Press, 1984.

Hoogenboom, Ari. *Rutherford B. Hayes: Warrior & President.* Lawrence: University Press of Kansas, 1995.

Kent, Zachary. Rutherford B. Hayes. Danbury, Conn.: Children's Press, 1989.

———. *The Civil War: "A House Divided."* Hillside, N.J.: Enslow Publishers, Inc., 1994.

Robbins, Neal E. *Rutherford B. Hayes: Nineteenth President of the United States.* Ada, Okla.: Garrett Educational Corporation, 1989.

Steins, Richard. *Hayes, Garfield, Arthur, & Cleveland.* Vero Beach, Fla.: Rourke Corporation, 1996.

Welsbacher, Anne. *Rutherford B. Hayes.* Edina, Minn.: ABDO Publishing Company, 2001.

Ziff, Marsha. *Reconstruction Following the Civil War in American History.* Berkeley Heights, N.J.: Enslow Publishers, Inc., 1999.

Index